Other Rom

DEREK MONG

saturnalia books

Saturnalia Books
105 Woodside Rd.
Ardmore, PA 19003
info@saturnaliabooks.com

ISBN: 978-0-9818591-8-7
Library of Congress Control Number: 2010939373

Book Design by Saturnalia Books
Printing by Westcan Printing Group, Canada

Cover Art: *Upright Image of the Coliseum inside Room # 23 at the Hotel Gladiatori, Rome,* 2008 by Abelardo Morrell.

Author Photograph by Ryan Mong

Distributed by:
University Press of New England
1 Court Street
Lebanon, NH 03766
800-421-1561

I would like to thank the editors of the following journals in which these poems originally appeared, occasionally in slightly different forms.

Alehouse; Artful Dodge; Cincinnati Review; Court Green; Crazyhorse; Devil's Lake Review; The Kenyon Review; Memorious; Michigan Quarterly Review; The Missouri Review; Pleiades; The Southeast Review; Third Coast; TriQuarterly; Yalobusha Review.

Additionally "Recoil" appeared on *The Missouri Review*'s website as the "Poem of the Week" and "Blackout" appeared on VerseDaily.org. "O h i o—" won the Grand Prize in the 2007 Happy Hour Poetry Awards from *Alehouse* and appeared in *Breathe: 101 Contemporary Odes* (C&R Press 2009). "Flying Is Everything I Imagine Now and More" appeared in *Love Rise Up* (Benu Press, 2011). "Coccyx" and "Octopus" were finalists for the *Southeast Review*'s Poetry Contest. "Thanatology" was the first runner-up for the Yellowwood Poetry Prize at *Yalobusha Review*. The poems appearing in *The Missouri Review* were awarded the Jeffrey E. Smith Editors' Choice Prize. An early portion of this book received the 2005 Hopwood Award in Poetry. The inestimable Laura MacDonald at Gaspereau Press released "Octopus" as a hand-set, hand-printed chapbook.

This book would not exist without the timely comments and frequent encourage-
ment of these writers and friends: David Baker, Ben Doyle, Laurence Goldstein,
Sarah Gorham, Linda Gregerson, Heather Jacobs, Jesse Lee Kercheval, Jennifer
Key, Jason Koo, Raymond McDaniel, Khaled Mattawa, John Miller, Wayne
Miller, Eric Parrish, D.A. Powell, Jeff Skinner, Kyle Thompson, Ann Townsend ,
Ron Wallace, and my Michigan MFA cohort. Thanks as well to the fine institu-
tions which offered me support and access to their exemplary students: the
University of Michigan and its Cornwell Fellowship, U of M's Hopwood Program
and Andrea Beauchamp, the Kenyon Review Young Writer's Workshop, The
Wisconsin Institute of Creative Writing and its Halls Poetry Fellowship,
Inkberry, the University of Louisville and its Axton Fellowship in Poetry, the
Edna St. Vincent Millay Society, Denison University and all the fine people at its
Jonathan R. Reynolds Young Writer's Workshop.

Thanks to Carl Phillips. Thanks to Abelardo Morrell for permission to use his
beautiful camera obscura photo. Thanks to Henry Israeli at Saturnalia Books for
his patience, dedication, and tireless work. Endless thanks to my wife Annie,
who—if she wasn't inspiring these poems—read them so well. And thanks to my
many families—in Dallas; Portland, OR; Waterford, MI; Ithaca, NY; San
Francisco; Tulsa; Davis, CA; Berkeley; and (here's to you Ryan) out with the
'great redtail' whose wing 'trailed under his talons when he moved.'

CONTENTS

❦

*This book is for my parents, Robert and Jean
and my wife, Anne Fisher*

FLYING IS EVERYTHING I IMAGINE NOW AND MORE

No shudder, no plunge, no cabin
                    strafed by sun

as when the earth constricts these wingtips and pulls
us like a bowstring
               below the cloudline; no
intercom or ice storm, no seatbelt signs lit

like a thought
            achieved in chorus; no red-eyes

trembling like cross hairs on the horizon;
no threat, no glance met
               (as has been endemic
these last ten years) by a fear that does nothing

but unite us—
          no flying really scares me

now save this scenario I've loved too long
and replayed
          at those altitudes where clouds still
canopy imagination: it begins

with the cabin pressure bled
             all over states

already red, till each passenger hovers,
tethered
        to their seat buckles or pursuing
chewing gum, their hands parting the breathing cups

like seaweed—

But stop. See my problem? I want

so badly to recast in-flight disaster
as gorgeous, that whoosh
                    of air narrowing where
an exit clasp detached and heaven gasps me

back into the ether,
                    even roll my limbs

in its mouth a spell before the earth draws back
on the distance

There's reason here, and a few good intentions

lost as this fall blurs
                    into the after-life

it's hurtling after: there's my plane sailing on,
there's its jetstream
                    of color-coded worry
trailing the tail-fin. I watch my clothes gently

lift away till I'm pale
                    as a lightning bolt

and the chutes of rain I've punched through nimbus clouds
chase me
                    toward the cause of all this desperate
imagination: it's these lit streets and crowds

looming larger now
                    and wholly literal

about all that they're afraid of. I once hoped

to ease the sky
                    within our reach, imagine
our brief victimhood as so much fuel burned up

in transit. But what can lyric
                              say to fear

hijacking countries? Only this, the lowest
point I can imagine:
                    I'm falling, arms out,
through smog, the dust splitting up till I'm costumed

in the exhaust
                    of my neighbors. I see cities

aglow like circuit boards, and cars lighting paths
from one target
                    to another. A noise lifts
skyward like a thousand screens, and I whisper

into that music:
                    America, I am

so harmless now, spilling down perpetually.
toward you. Draw
                    your sunroofs back and call me
home. Let your grass blades raise their heads to meet me.

OCTOPUS

Monterey, 2004

*

. His flesh stretched out in eight squirmy tails

        or so my cousin Natalie, she's six today, believes—

Look, look, I can see his feelers! I can touch his suckers!

O octopus, my umber then amber bundle, will you fill your parachute

      (now you're chartreuse)—and teach me how to hide

               when everyone is looking?

Nat, too smart for six, told me once that *dolor* rhymes with color

                     also feelers   also lover.

*

Sunday morning, ten AM—

        my love and I munch marshmallow cereal

in bed—   I scatter a handful across her belly   then slowly, almost wholly

kiss away the constellation.

Here is my confession: surprised by sudden love I am equally unsure of where in time we are or might

be going: by noon she's red as every sixth bit of cereal,   the color

of our coming.

*

Natalie again, perfectly enamored: *did you know they funnel water?*

It's true. It's called a siphon.

She's right. It works like jet propulsion: octopi don't so much

move as occupy another burst of ocean—

call it piggybacking streams, Technicolor flush, a dance, or drift,

just register my envy: my flesh will always displace a place—

the octopus is

wherever it is going—

*

To feel is not the same, nor even analogous, to having feelers—

and yet both, through subterfuge and hues, rely upon

the palette: some days I'm blue and lightly bruised, conspicuous as the ocean.

Tomorrow I will redden, let passion

fog my picture.

My love—

are we ever more than our collected strokes

of pain or pleasure? I want so badly to breathe

*

clear   across my canvas, maybe cast it into a pane

of glass and live inside, transparent

as six-year-old adulation: *I can see him! I can see him! I can touch*

his feelers! Eye to eye, Nat and the octopi, she fogs

the glass like a dragon,

even draws a star (five points for the cephalopod) around

a sucker: this is how we stare into the glass

without facing our reflection.

*

Monterey, some beach, this summer:

           as my lover disappears behind the reeds to pee

I realize that, despite the moonlight, she's the absence

                of color: her skin is steam—

      her hair's the evening air: deep black and absorbing.

Tonight the tide will swell with jellyfish, translucent.

If I am silent, still as the dunes themselves,

             I swear that she will never reach me.

          *

Look, you can see it moving—

       Nat is pressed so close to the glass I cannot,

   at first, make out

         the ink cloud, spreading thin as conversation

    through the water. *Neat trick* she says, and I agree

      as the octopus disappears, his body like a fogged-in flare

shot up   from the bottom of the ocean.

   I am green with envy.

*

I am seen

        by anyone and everyone

willing to pull the ink away and part its curtain.

    Natalie is miffed, proceeds to tap the glass and ask: *Why did he go away?* I offer that *he might be shy*, but am thinking

        four limbs plus four limbs   equals a couple.

    She is unimpressed, instead suggests:

        Can we go feed the seagulls?

Equivalents

Concerning equivalents:
                    lost amid
the Roman catacombs, a priest will halve
his candle flame
                    until one glow doubles
and redoubles on the tongues of terra-
cotta pots—
            a lesson the split earthworm

learns, as he stands twice the chance of being
split again:
            a wise move to reproduce
for two worms slither twice as far as one,
which explains
            why warheads unlock themselves
above a cityscape, thus brokering

a wider
        higher bloom—
                    their sanguine hues

and party stars spread throughout the ether.
Are scant survivors
                what this division
equals? How does such backwards algebra
apply to the holy
                whose wafers, cracked
in eighths, constitute a body, though whole

ones add up to crackers? Furthermore, how
am I standing here,
                by-product of bi-
furcating cells, each one teased in two till
too many pulls
            spelled *embryo*, and one
final tug divided *me* from *mother*?

Recoil

I taste it every time—
                thick as a pool

of diesel fuel or varnish, smooth as smoke Os
rolling tarnish
            down my tonsils, a slow one
wreathes my tongue—God, how I love the air inside

a room that wields a gun;
                it makes the air taste

better. Watch the body's possibilities
increase
          by one, then two: first as victim, then
assassin. The first time I felt a firearm

neither shot nor shoot
              were options: the barrel,

bolt and butt were scattered like a crime scene. Some-
one had dismantled it, hidden
             half under
the guest bedroom's box springs. My brother simply

fished the barrel out,
           then plugged his thumb into

the butt end, cramming red paper, bouquet-style,
out from the muzzle.
           He brushed my face, shouted
bang! then punched me in the stomach. It would be

years before I shot one:

I'm splayed out sniper-

style and sighting a single bowling pin at
fifty yards. The first shot
                    bucked my forearm up—
the gun's butt stamped a bruise into my cheekbone,

a powder burn, a watermark.
                    How could I

cleanse it without now igniting more powder?
I learned then that whatever magic
                         bullets
enact with their one thought—*keep moving*—the hand

still recalls
              the reaction: ghost round, shadow

slicing through the shooter. Its only trace: ash
crisping the nostrils,
                    sometimes a tinny spin,
not music, not crackling, washing the eardrums.

Its truth: I am alive.
                    Its lie: I can breathe

equal parts sex and danger. To this day I'm
weak to its
              seduction: a whisper will slip
from the goose-gun over my best friend's mantle—

a cabinet's rifles and pistols
                    stand up

like organ pipes, muffled. Once, I woke up drunk
at a girlfriend's house and found
                              instead of aspirin
a black six-shooter. It was unloaded, cold,

and as I rolled it cowboy style
                        down my thigh,

then pointed the muzzle into the mirror—
I felt myself more naked,
                              small, while the world
grew more heightened: the bathmat's hairs split my toes

with moisture; I saw the wall
                        paint flaking off

like eucalyptus. I knew, without looking,
the morning had warmed
                              colorless, and she would
love me right through it. I let the pistol swing,

limp from the pivot
                        of my finger. Its sight

tapped the glass. I swung gently from its trigger.

FELLINI'S CABIRIA

released May 26, 1957

Dear Reader: can we dispense with introductions? Your ready ears
drew me here, your patience will retain me. Let's have dinner, see a movie
(ok, this one's a love story), maybe trade whispers in my favorite formal verse:
the sestina. It's true, I take my poems to the pictures, hold their sheets up to the screen,
let films rewrite them! Barthes explains with this moviegoer motto: *inclusum labor
illustrat!* or "enclosed I work and glow!" Ergo, we can both review

these words by light cast from our buttered fingers. So to begin, *vide* this view
of our heroine: Cabiria, call-girl with whopping vaudeville eyes, button ears,
stands hypnotized. She's swooning. (*Nota Bene:* I skip around, cuts down on labor
costs, duration). Still, remember this: you're two acts into a dim movie's
darkest, dirty *notti*. You're verging on cinema's seduction—a screen
will brood in muted hues, then turn the corner lightly. Ex.: the hypnotist reverses

Cabiria's fortunes. She meets a man (*chiamo Oscar!*), they drink, converse,
then walk into the sunlit ever-after. I told you, it's a love story, a view
so skewed you can't help but cheer her. Or is it a love story between our screen
selves and their happy endings? Dear Reader: point that projector at my ear
and watch its light slice through my irises (they're mini-movie
slides) until my eyes kaleidoscope their labors

and pipedreams. Watch my rented room assume a film lab's
sun, it's a Technicolor lampshade! My lover flies us to Spain, Spielberg options my verse
for his next movie. I retire at thirty. I've reason to imagine this: Fellini's movie
ends at twilight, the outdoor analogue for the movie viewer's
hypnosis (Barthes again, swooning). Watch Oscar rob her, run. Watch the tears
appear. Cue the moonlight. So is Fellini positing, via the big screen,

a commentary on sappy movies? Is silver gelatin a tramp, running screens
from eye to gut to groin; she leaves your pockets bare, skin belabored,
filmy. I daresay this calls for more poems. Come one, come all! Let's fill those ears
with the same six words (*Ok, it is a love story*) and turn this verse
form into the new hypnotic pastime! Dear Reader, it's this easy: I obstruct your view
by standing inside the projector's eye. I'm making shadows. I'm moving

into moving pictures and you're feeling very, very sleepy. *NB*: our movie's
nearly run its course and yet nobody's kissed. Must be trouble with the screen-
play. Let's rewrite it. Enter *You* onto an Italian street, Dutch angle. My view-
finder finds your droopy eyes; manholes steam, extras mull, an elaborate
backdrop frames you. What lover are you waiting for? Is your dream's inverse
(longing in a movie in a poem) worth chasing? I zoom in, you hear

footsteps, a shadow slips into your movie. You've exactly 39 lines to elaborate
on a single thought: *ok, I love you*. I'll dim the lights, I'll dip the screen in silver, revers
the viewfinder. Look inside, recite: *Dear Cabiria, Dear Reader—*

SPECULATION

Have I cornered you, my self, again—
Hiding inside this red-washed face, below

The curtain of our hair? Do you mind
If I clear an oval in the mirror and show

My face your face vignetted in the steam?
Can we now reconcile my fear that you

Exist but ostensibly, ghost on the bathroom
~~Wall whose pupils eclipse when I construe~~

Words for the stuff reflected in the frame?
Showerhead, spigot mount, Juniper shampoo—

Each breath fogs the mirror, we déjà vu
Again. Suppose then we agree on steam

Between our mouths, breathe clouds through
Which our tongues cross, kiss, and turn

The expression of our likenesses into
Something as analogous as names.

So sit still. Exhale. Mimic the man who
Stares you down and watch his eyes widen

Like holes you're falling through. You know
Two words to halt it all: *You do?* No. I am.

Coccyx

for Annie

Less bone than musket
ball, yet poised enough to pause
on a china plate:

the sacrum. My love,
you'd rather roll *tailbone* off
your tongue; it claims both

purpose and absence.
Last night, folding my hand like
a leaf inside your

hands, you led us both
right where the animal self
extended: I touched

that bump, fulcrum of
your shadow side, which, apart
from mirrors, pictures,

you're incapable
of glimpsing. I rubbed you till
it gave off light, light

like the static that
leaps from flannel: Oh my sweet,
is this your anchor—

three to five caudal
vertebrae your spine has hitched
its rigging to while

your skull lulls on, all
portholes open? You are al-
ready asleep; I'm

getting close, can see
dream's underwater fiefdom—
it's there we'll wear our

body's obverse, skin
like pairs of slacks we've put on
backwards. For once I'll

reach my past before
my present, the days lined up
like prizefighters, floored

before I touch them.
Can you see our legs unlace,
maybe walk away,

though our eyes never
stop meeting? Will we stumble
together again

two blind vagabonds
traversing the equator—
arms outstretched, searching

for that bell, that bone,
the coccyx? When I turn on-
to my side tonight

ours touch, exert some
force, lode-stone like, though we know
they're not load-bearers.

Vitruvian Man

Dear symmetric bloke, Mr. Hub and Spoke, what is desire
But a lack between physiques: as in yours, classic specimen
Of men, and mine, i.e. a body? Must extremities measure

Regular as pillars, fit in patterns, or can we consider
My scars, my stutter sexy? I am a creature of incompletion,
Made asymmetric, broke, my limbs speak of what desire

They haven't tasted: my flesh wallows, yours knows flavors.
Do you think Leonardo drew you as an emblem, the one
Man whose body proves (*in extremis*) that man's the measure

Of all things, or should we conclude that all things, whether
Man, muscle-width, or lust can be measured? Did he hear Reason,
That symmetric bloke, Mr. Humble croak: *this is desire*—

"No Man's torso (i.e. 6 palms) will exceed his shoulders?"
Are you a harpsichord, a star, or the most rhetorical of questions?
No man's mind, eyes, or bodies' extremities will measure

Up to your standards. Like most people I will hover
Between plague and pollination, thus tumbling from, unstrung,
Your dear geometric block, Mr. Hub and Spoke, my desires
Mended, mindful. I will sing of bodies, extremities, and measures.

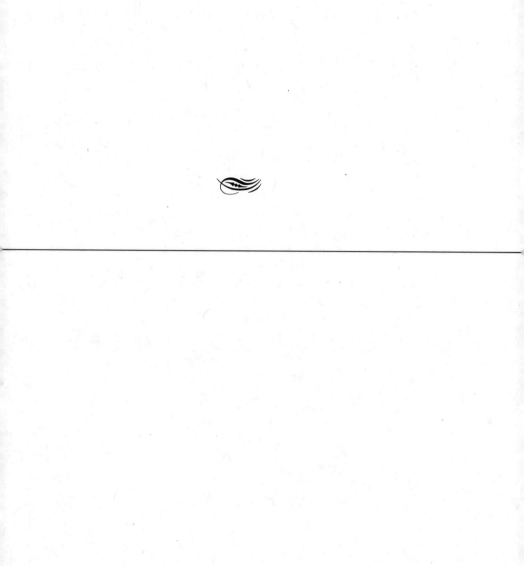

Songs of Sickness

I. His Doctor, His Fever

after Johannes Kreihing

For this I am sorry—
mine is a sad tale, common to the tongues
of our poor:
        it begins after supper

when my chest blushes then goosebumps
as if I'd swallowed
               stove coals
or locusts.

Therefore, I sit down to pray:

      Dear God, had you thought me
      a furnace, shouldn't I bear wrought-iron
      arms,
              and skin that would sing
      to the strike of a mallet?

And yet I wake
to winter and summer struggling
inside me: my fingertips
              numb as tombstones—
all ten can't hold
my head up, hot as a twice-shot cannonball.

Again, I sit down to pray:

      Dear God, our Father—
      Why send me
            this doctor, his one cure

is a blessing he whispers
from my navel to my shoulders:
Your soul, my son, will live through the day—

I have no relief.

II. Song of Songs 5.6

after Matthias Sarbiewski

So you'll know me, My Lord, I have dismantled
   my body and released it, piece by piece,
through the branches and stars. This is what I call love.
   My heart I unveiled, and it flew off like a sparrow,
but my heart, dear Christ, you did not return.
   My will I released as one would a firm handshake,
but my will never reached your knocker, your door.
   ~~My mind you've kept like an inkwell near the window.~~
My breath feeds your candles, your lamps. Now I fold
   my soul up for its journey, which, if you wear it,
will render me naked, and like a living corpse I will stay.

III. A Priest to Paul Russus,
The Stupid Old Man Who Still Longs for Money

after Jacob Masen

Look here, we've another
      old codger, this one picking
  a sixpence from the curb.
    Don't you see

that sewer, Paul Russus,
      smell the stench
  you've trundled into? Better get
    used to the view,

old man. The underworld's
      waiting just under that grate.
  Tell me, tell your
    savior, why do you bother

with coins, when your skin
      hangs in husks, its folds barely
  hide your ripening corpse?
    See those wrinkles, heavy

as netting, beneath each
      eyelid, feel that beard, white
  as frost with only six teeth
    poking through?

I know you bottle
      those coins up in your basement.
  Is their clatter the one sound
    to pass

through your waxed-up ears?
       Russus, I think you fooled
    Death long ago,
      and are surviving

in fractions: the nervous
       tick, that low tide you call
    a hairline, the icicles in your nose.
    Why not abandon

that sixpence before
      you're no more
    than a bottle's worth
      of body? Leave me enough flesh

to perform your last rites.

IV. Phillip Nerius Moderates Ambition with Two Words

after Giacomo Lubrani

Today, these streets
teem with soothsayers and slim
pamphlets. Recently I met

a priest who leveled a forest
so he could pack his pillows with sawdust.
Last night, I heard the learned

stuff their shirts with loose
pages. Don't they know
they too will catch cold; they'll sneeze?

Sickness takes no heed
of distinction, and the laws written
yesterday will still answer

to the question, *What then?*
Only the public dancers, twirling
their braids and bracelets

can take their trade with them:
each limb spins itself into ashes,
each ash heap dances,

partnered to the wind—
What then?

V. The Tomb of the Dying Year

after Vincenzo Guiniggi

Careful where you stand, and be sure
to step lightly—
                I am like your shadow
buried shallow,

those boot soles shake the weed roots
that brush my nose.

My only crime was increasing
the life
                of each human, though some say

I am punished for passing
Christ's birthday
                        without pause—
I admit it: I let night
stitch its blanket over your day.

Still, I would have you remember
I am not angry,
                for my death spreads out
so sweetly
                beneath the earthwork—

my tomb is Christ's cradle;
my chest is a place for your feet.

As for my grief, I will wear it
like a pearl necklace,
                        how else to explain

these fields of dew?

At the Johnsonville Bratwurst Eating Competition— Sheboygan, Wisconsin, 2006

Gentlemen, let's prep our guts
                              for uncut sausage links,
fan bibs beneath our chins, then turn to the Jumbo-Dog-
A-Tron (it burps
                    every rich minute down) and wait
for the tale of the plate to thunder through our stomachs—
its moral is simple:
                    in America so much

world can be understood as fits down your gullet, or
if we translate into our sponsor's speech—
                                        start EATING!
And a rush of teeth shakes the stage, and beer foam cascades
from paper cups, while somewhere
                              a paramedic waits
smoking Camels. But you, dear Reader, you know today

won't take the cake for wastage—
                              however fast we mash
brats into our maws, however quick the announcer's
wit (*these meatheads*
                    sure can hot dog!) no one's quite outpaced
the metaphor an eating bout presents for our coast-
to-coast approach (sixty seconds down!)
                                        to abundance:

let's consume it! Imagine each of these sausages
is an old growth pine
                    and we've gnawed away ocean views
for half of California. Or picture them as mile-
posts, as railroad ties
                    and we've crossed the prairie twice (eight
minutes left!) and still been hungry. You'd think this thought might

lend us pause, but give a man a bucketful
                              of brats,

and he won't just eat for a day, he'll find there's nothing
he can't swallow.
                        Sure, folks starve for lack of what will stain
our shirts, and the Brits build cars that run like cordless (five
minutes of brat love left!) toasters.
                        And I've traveled there.

And I've come home to a TV on, my sprinklers wet,
and highways I'll follow
                        toward a shopping plaza.
Nothing felt any more out of place than fifty states
and a gas station
                        on every corner. Which explains
why I'm sitting beside a bald guy who once out-ate

a bear and he's pulling past
                        (two minutes left!) the teen
who can almost digest marbles, and I've stopped chewing—
for if excess
                        is in my blood, if Wal-Mart followed
a path blazed by the wagon train, then I might as well
enjoy it.
                        So let's focus now on the Jumbo-Tron.

Let's watch bear man go for bulk or broke (thirty seconds
left!) and forget how far we've come
                        from kosher. Let's watch
the screen divide, zoom down on these mouths, dark as dueling
oubliettes above us.
                        Kids wave foam fingers bearing
their favorite eater's name; the screen tells us "Size Matters

When It's Your Stomach!" then starts (five!)
                        the final countdown.
Let's remember (four!) the stakes today: one golden brat,
one lifetime
                        supply (three!) of hot dogs. Let's join the crowd
in ridiculing (two!) the loser: *hey snack-attack!*
Hey ya bite-size chump! (one!) *Go eat*
                        (we're done!) *your heart out!*

A-Fib

lives inside this lie:

heartbeats simply sync
up the body's clock

and repeat in one
direction. Truth is,

like two boots in snow
retracing their tracks,

every ticker tip-
toes over ground once

covered, till each beat
flips to face what path

it's tread and sprints home-
sick toward beginning—

marking, as comets
do, its pinnacle

by all it burns off
in turning. The skin

grows hot, cooks layers
it forgot to shed,

till the flesh is lens
our blood pools under

like a stoplight sunk
into the body,

a rewinding so
gaudy it blinds us

to the future, days
of which simply drift

away unnoticed,
beats we bargained off

for a less distant
dark and this thought, small

enough to carry:
between two unknown

points the shortest walk
is always the one

already traveled.

FELLINI'S SATYRICON

released March 11, 1970

Fast forward to Trimalchio, the sausage platter shot, then scroll
through the special features. Can we slow-mo the banquet scene
just when the meat explodes and its greasy bits speckle the stage players,
Nubians, and albino maître d'? *Nota Bene:* a certain exotic Other-
ness marks Fellini's cast of extras. Consult the shooting script for insight
into this mixed company, what the Romans called *farrago*

and we translate as hodge-podge or cattle fodder and go
about our merry way. In Nero's day the entertainment came scroll-
bound, snapped into hexameters, and set for court poets to recite.
Enter Titus Petronius, the *elegantiae arbiter* and author seen
by Nero's ministers as a nemesis, culture snob, or seedy bard whose other
talents remained satiric, from the Latin *satura*, perhaps a play

on *satyr*, though Braund, et al. contend this etymology plays
too heavy on the Greek. Turn then to Juvenal, who coins *farrago*
(see I.86, trans. above) to describe his little books of verse, though other
Latin scribes provide variant etymologies. In Diomedes' remaining scrolls
he defines *satura* (think saturate) as "a sausage eaten during religious scenarios,
the insides stuffed with various ingredients," a line cited

from Varro, ergo *quid est satura?* Rewind now. Fellini's on site
in Rome, canvassing the carnivals for a hundred human oddities to play
Roman demigods and generals. *Nota Bene*: In the Ceres Temple scene
a *lecta* (trans. "carriage") wobbles on the burly arms of six *spago*[1]
as they herald the "Hero of the Battle of Quadragesimo," a role
given to a quadruple amputee (see *satura*). Don't bother

to trace this shot, excess from the fragment of a tale that's other-
wise non-narrative.[2] Better to blame Petronius whose unsightly
suicide (wrists slit, sewn up, then slit, see Tacitus) left the scrolls
of the *Satyricon* to the worms. The undigested parts became a play-
ground of forms: prose novel, picaresque odyssey, a *farrago*
of verse. Scholars stitch it up, trim the fray, but like Hollywood scenery

the fake clouds still look fake. So with what we've seen
what have we learned? *Conclusion*: fractured texts are other-
worldly, the classics "a nebulous galaxy"³ where brave men go
to die. *Questions for future analysis*: How do I cite
the booklet for my DVD? Should your average screenplay
include all, *a lá* the sausage chain, or is *The Satyricon* just bloated scrawl?

1. The *spago* (trans. eunuch) scene was never scripted, but shot (a total fluke) on-site.
2. Would you work to adapt the work of another? Do I own a film when I press PLAY?
3. Costanzo Costantini's *Conversations with Fellini*. Go to *Film, Italy*, or *Satire's Role*.

OHIO—

an etymology

        comes to us from *oh hello*
Which some believe to mean "I am in a state
Of abbreviated greeting," i.e.: she blinks, I wave,
She winks before the Erie snow

Can melt upon my glasses. Other Ohio
Examples: gravel strafed by headlights, a shield
Of green seen from a cockpit. Explanation two
~~Contends Ohio grew into a double ode~~

From a sole, initial blooper: *uh oh*—
Oh oh, oh ooooh my home can speed into a love
Cry or a lyric! Is such ecstasy dubious
when its first note foreshadows

Its finale? Like army time, zeroes
Frame all of Ohio's encounters. Some even think
We split off from a whisper which went creasing
Through the prairie: *I ow a— O hi o*—

Sisters till a glacier cleaved them? Oh
No, not so. Ohio's as indivisible as amber waves
From rusted pickups. In fact, I've traced
My state's origin back to this abiding sorrow:

It's night, I'm driving with my windows
Down, the cold's encircling my collar. I swear
The earth below me begins to swell and drop
Like three syllables stretched into four low

Then lower letters. The sky goes blank with snow.
I drove and drove into the pages of Ohio.

Blackout

Little blue bolt on a split wire—
shock in the dark, my corrupter

       of clocks—

you quiver once then kindle flames
that lick the bark off evergreens,

       one's broken bough

unbound you from your artery,
so blow the grid and burn the tree

       till block by block the dark

will dawn along these gravel roads
and cars crawl home on the harness

of their highbeams. Let the tiki

torches dot the lawns. Let screen doors
swing with laughter and lukewarm beer.

       Next door

my neighbors cuss the curfew cop,
someone shoots Roman candles off

       their roof and cheers.

I'm home, upstairs, stripped to nothing
but my underwear and running

       in the dark. My lips part—

I plunge into the emptiness
where a bed should be, its mattress

the net beneath an acrobat

blindfolded, free: my fall is like
the time it takes a match to strike

> and singe

the sheets: I am a comet streak
or spark. I will end incomplete.

FELLINI'S ROMA

released October 11, 1972

Its History *& Origin*	is strictly fiction, the gist of which is this: Rome's a Roman candle blown smoldering over a timeline. Big parts burn off, we reorder the cinders into a story, maybe whip up a recipe to best exemplify the *urbs* *aeterna*: add wolf's milk to Mussolini musk. Sprinkle with papacy. Simmer. Guides often disguise the mishmash that is Roma. Not Fellini! This film locates itself inside the director's eye, but runs laps along his iris. Some FAQs: "wh‹
Transportation *& Traffic:* *No One Curbs* *Their Horses*	will Fellini, my portly Vergil, take me? Will the *You Are Here* stickers at St. Peter's be in English or Latin?[*]" Though this author skipped R‹ Roma's traffic was so bad, taillights glowed in his oatmeal. The locals will remind you Caesar outlawed horsecarts before sunset, proof this disor‹ grows from two millenia of improper urban planning. To avoid congestion hir guides, rent motorbikes, and drive the *Raccordo Annulare* (it links the six *suburbi*)
Accomodations: *Hotels,* *Brothels,* *or Necropoli*	till you're orbiting the city. Fellini did, filmed drivers encircling the *urbs* *Saturnis*, their faces bathed in stoplight, exhaust, thoughts drifting where- ever they recall quiet, *vino*. Better to walk. Better let the *Via delle Carozze* gui‹ you toward accommodations. Stay in Keats' room (a museum now), visit Ron brothels and necropoli. Both have extended rates and leave their boarders speechless. We offer coupons to anyone who can locate
Restaurant *Reconnaissance:* *Pizza or* *Piazza?*	the housing conceived exclusively for Romans![†] Redeem them at local restaurants, or Fellini's gastrointestinal inferno. More disturb- ing than the movie's papal fashion show remains the food ordered on the Piazza. Bring a loose belt, a bib: to see such meat will leave your underwear distended. Likewise the diners' mantra: "In Rome whatever you eat turns to shit," so let's feast upon the screen and guide

our hunger toward popcorn, soda. Here are some handy guide-
lines for viewings or visits. 1) during *Roma* one man wanders among the locals,
actors, tourists. *Vide* Federico Fellini! Like God or the Tiber's aroma
he both flows through and hovers over this city. 2) While inside the urban
limits avoid getting arrested, and (this one's important) 3) Wherever
you go in Rome, do as the Romans do, unless disorder's

raining down and they're getting sacked by Vandals. It's a tall order
stemming from a simple reason: Roman jurisprudence. Any smart guide-
book highlights its sluggishness, finding metaphors everywhere
for its victims (*vide* these ruins). To end, some trivia questions: What local
district built the *Barofonda Theatre*? Can you name (*in Italiano!*) Rome's 35
urban
sectors?‡ Do the movie's motorbikes really rev up with *roma, roma, roooooma*!?

ANSWERS to FAQs & Trivia:
like Fellini's runway nuns, *Roma* wears many hats, speaks in both dead and dancing languages. † Early suburban sprawl guided Roman masons toward the *insula* (apart-ment), providing the ‡local *quartieri urbani* some order.

ON THE HILLS OF PERUSIA

after Propertius I.21 & I.22

Gallus

As when a smattering of cinders
flips a stable
                            to stampede,
or a name, the whiff
of grain recalls a good day, its shade—

so too do rumors
convulse these ramparts.
                                        You there,
fleeing but unwounded: bend
down to this grass and sandal grit, lift

my voice toward your ear—

    I have a sister named Acacia.
    I have wounds enough to prove I slipped

through Caesar's lines. Tell her
there's a ribcage waiting

amid this rubble. Tell her
to rebuild me with twice as many bones.

Propertius

Judge me by my family, or even the gods
    sleeping on my mantel—I no longer care. My past
is like a shadow, thinning when the sun plunges
    under those hills. There's dust frosting the tops
of Perusia; there are Roman bones dispersed
    like dinner scraps, as if Jove gorged himself on legions.
At night they drum their femurs on the hot, dry ground,
    testing for reentry. My cousin's there, unburied.
Climb that hillside, listen for his whispering,
    his teeth still free from dirt. As for your question—
I was born in Umbria, a fertile land, with horses.

MIA

b. 2-18-2005

Little unclothed
    émigré, did you know
        that after this first day
    a sleep will sink

the bridge
    your body makes
        between your former
    shores and our

unanswered questions?
    So lie still, maybe catch my eye—
        I would like
    to read your pupils,

delicate as candle wicks,
    before they fill your irises
        with color. Will their wells
    tell me if you've begun

yet to remember?
    Do you think I'll see in them
        our shared family, either
    the hundreds

we've both surged
    like beach surf from—
        or these tears, the love
    you traded up for?

Somewhere in the shadows
    there, you also know
        what thought is like
    before thought tells you

its thinking. Please, for years
        I've breathed this air
                but have never reached
        an answer. Do you hear

birds lifting from and returning
        to a fountain, perhaps
                a faucet dripping? My head
        has shed that sound,

its meaning. Once when left
        alone inside a hotel room,
                I tried to recreate it—
        one mirror, my best

blank stare, the refrain
        of my name coming from—
                I swore this was so—
        the reflection. The night

was still, the room cool
        as a tuning fork,
                but still I knew
        that I was

thinking. Sometimes
        I apply the opposite
                logic, wrap my head
        inside thought's riverbed

and turn on the water—
        Still, such abundance leads
                no more to origins
        than to your recent

shore: its absence.
        Mia, it will be years
before I meet you.

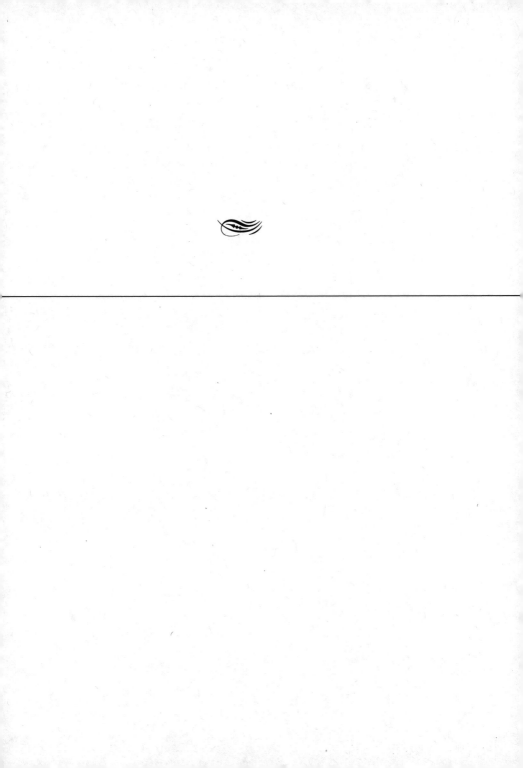

Morning, Noon, and Night

1.

Today's nothing
       but sun, white
       curtains flung
           till their shadows span

our feet. Last week
       (did I tell
       you this?) I
           found an old woman

asleep in our
       tomatoes.
       She lay there
           as you now drowse here,

though this weekend's
       pace slips like
       a glacier
           between us. Listen—

that's our world gone
       on working:
       somewhere tree
           branches tap their pane

of glass, the street
       hums and stills—
       your kettle
           begins to tremble.

Everywhere grief
       figures it-
       self inside
           this house so long as

we lock our doors
        to all that
        keeps breathing
                through our one keyhole.

2.

Noon, hotter: You
        sneak inside
        the *Times*, munch
                toast, eggs, tomatoes.

I drift between
        my dreams and
        these headlines,
                unsure which I am

more afraid of
        skimming, pain
        I will close
                my eyes to, or pain

I can just smear
        with fingers.
        Yesterday
                a girl walked into

the fog; we wash
        our mugs while
        the cops go
                looking for her boy-

friend. Tomorrow
        the gulf will
        spite the poor
                some more, a lost war

just continues.
        When you reach
        the shower
                steam, I pause at each

of our windows,
        breathe clouds in-
        to the glass
                until I'm followed

by vanishing
        ellipses.
        Your garden
                brims in their absence.

3.

Is the trouble
        that our world's
        troubles reign
                large, or that we love,

guilt-free, above
        them? You've heard
        me leave you
                asleep, ease myself

into the gray
        light that leaks
        from midnight
                movies, but sometimes

I simply drive,
        swing my head-
        lights till they
                skim the river's edge,

then wade in up
        to my belt-
           line. It's there
                I caught a water-

strider, cupped him
        inside the
        high beam's light
                and watched grace sustain

itself, a grace
        so untouched
        by all that
                pressure it thrives on.

4.

Tonight's nothing
        but love, stripped
        clothes, pillows
                spilling massacred

from the sofa.
        Moonlight fills
        the pots and
                pans, we pass our hands

along the bridge
        these hips in-
        sinuate
                between us. Is there

one whisper here,
        two, or three
        when I speak
                of the old woman—

how she woke, seeds
       like acne
       on her chin,
           to my one question:

Do you want some
       tomatoes?
       Eyes closed, breath
          low, I try to sleep

beside you, washed
       by your breath's
       lonely hum—
          it moves, a buoy

through the evening.

TO MY OLDER SIBLING, MISCARRIED

Forestalled one,
                bracketed in absences,

why does your sleep still stir an echoing
on nights my mother calls
                   and has nothing
to say? Was it there, fluent through the phone's

black holes,
              I heard you disappear, either

whisked into some other womb or recalled
by the wake-less,
               some darkness that welcomed
you to plague our mother with sleeplessness—

your face and fingertips
                mining her dreams

like ingrown hairs? Often I envy you,
first cut from my father's
                 mold, yet wholly
expectationless. Why are you always

male?
        We met thirteen years back, the evening

my dad took me to the Health Museum
and explained exactly how it went
                       wrong—
one man, one boy circled by nine female

mannequins whose bellies
               were wide glass balls

ballooning month by month. The display was
called the "Panorama
                         of Pregnancy"
and in a voice that said *you're old enough*

my father read
                   the paneling and pressed

a button, acknowledging *It was there—*
blue light, fifth ball from the right,
                                          you were pale.
I held my forehead to the cold fluorescence

until it hummed, till it pulsed
                                  with your voice.

PATHETIC FALLACY

A clipped nail swept from the windowsill,
beard crumbs circling the drainpipe: every

      day

the world whisks another trace of me
away and weaves it into a bird's

      nest, crowning

its longevity with my walking,
inconstant harvest. Look close, you'll note

      its taunting: some scrub grass

my tennis shoes mashed simply bounces
back, while the earth dances its next lap—

shakes one more year out of my column.

Worse yet, the landscape behind my eyes
is equally deceitful. It's there

      my old selves call me back

like bats, till I'm no more than echoes
rebounding, an ever fainter trace

      of person-

hood fringing the memories I'm meant
to constitute and visit. Between

      two

collapsing fields my voice runs its zipper.
For years I've launched this body forward.

To Keep From Drowning

Madison, Wisconsin

Think of your latch-lock's
pendulum in the doorframe; think
of sun soaking the hardwood floors today till napping
felt like falling upwards—
and think of ice rising through
lakes that flank this town like eyeglasses cut from water.
Now walk down Tenney Pier to confront
your guilt before
winter anchors it beneath a snowdrift. There you'll re-
call your grandmother, who—widowed
by husband number
three—trailed petals, stems, and pruning shears through a house filled
with as many casseroles
as flowers. Remember
her one question: *Can they cremate me in my greenhouse?*
Nothing growing made much sense
to her, and though you'd flown
out to play board games and reheat meals, her only joy
was cutting down whatever wilted.
Small joy indeed—
at dusk her dog walked you further from the house, her grief
so thick you both breathed
gentler on its fringes. *Write this
down one day*, she said. And here's the guilty part: you hid
for hours at the dead man's desk
doing exactly that
while his grandchildren, his son, watched you from their pictures.
You leave that feeling
by the rocks where the geese feed.
You think of why we return to nature ceaselessly—
not for what it says to us
but what we abandon

at its wayside. Your mother understood this when you
once prolonged a fight
                              to prove you argued civilly
in public. This made you strangers for her trip's short time,
a distance that didn't dissipate
                              till she rose in-
to a jet-stream, and you returned to making weekly
phone calls. This you'd learn distilled you
                                          to a man who'd need
no one to visit him in this old Midwestern town
where every highway fans out elsewhere.
                                    And your lover's
at the end of a longer one, pushing through this year
apart. Think of her tonight.
                          Think of the child she'd bring
to your ever smaller world if you'd only agree
waiting for the perfect time
                              means waiting forever.
You wonder now why you hold her back, afraid perhaps
that whatever point
                      three people form will send your life,
arrow-like, down a path you're not sure you can manage.
You think you're still young.
                          You know you'll miss the luxury
of being selfish. Think of the time she could have said
to you *if you slip through this wave*
                              with me, your body
will not wet a drop, and you'd have believed her. That was
eighteen months ago. She wore
                              a shawl, no shoes, had lived
across the globe but never walked in the Pacific.
Your lives then were not your own, but
                                    shot so far into
the blue sky, the present seemed like one more roll of film

you hadn't yet developed.
                              Now you both write upon
the edge of separate lakes, plotting your split lives in
unison like chess moves.
                              So think of your local
bar. Think of the water you drink by the glass and that
glib response
                              you offer your friends when they ask why:
to keep from drowning. You leave their laughter here. You leave
everything
                              in your pockets. Walk down your lampless street.
Listen to the second floors. Now think of home and how
your neighbor
                              shouts her kids to bed before wrapping her-
self in a flatscreen's thunder. Tonight you'll wait awhile
before asking if she'll please
                              be quiet. You think of
her eyes, darting inside their recent dose, as she lists
her daily woes, replete
                              with anecdotes and exact
amounts. These are designed to keep you from returning.

THANATOLOGY

insists on gripping *death*
                    like a semantic
wishbone, then bending our end word till its great
beyond (to be
                    dead) splits from those nearly gone
(the long dying) and a space pervades, which we
slip questions through,
                    listening for an echo:
must the body (call it x) sustain a brain-
stem (that's y)
               ~~or can the two die mutually~~
exclusive? Does x mark where our being stops?
Do we hope our *ys*
                repot like exotic
flowers? Meanwhile our hands retie *death's* double-

meaning. This word's nothing if not metaphor—
say *death* and bleed
                 two opposites together:
sayonara meets silent night, our big sleep's
swept into a swan song.
                 Doctors like limits
well-defined, and their lives are spent listening
to patients edge them. But who's felt
                 a pulse fade
like a smoldered cigarette, or just slipped out-
side, smoked one quick,
                 and missed a loved one's drifting?
Cold as the stethoscope's probe, much as it hears
inside, our bodies spend lifetimes
                 learning their

erasing game. You're never going to catch them.

Period

Cicero, In L. Catilinam Oratio Prima 254 – 258

July 2005: as regards
                two Humvees crisped

like matchboxes on CNN, leading a congressman
to claim, and with the same voice
                         he taped six months ago,
that the meaning of this loss will become evident

if we hold out one more year—
                  I too wish none of it

were true, for what are we to do when the language
of the state begins to ape (it flirts
                    toward all it lacks)
the language of seduction? *We won't leave until this*

darn job is done, sounds less like a duty than a death
sentence—
            Period! And though they wrote
the war's cause off, the hawks still garner faithful legions.

Autumn 63 BC:
            M. Tulli, quid agis?—

Cicero, Roman consul this year, begins to speak
in *impersonatio*, his voice
               hangs from a leash
within his grasp, feigns the Republic's tone, then turns

a question on its master. Neither his answer

nor the query now matter,
save that Catiline's response
must be guessed at in the margins, and the State's sentence

(it translates subject,
blood and verb) knots its clauses

noose-like, delays its winnowed meaning: read period.
What writer wouldn't be seduced, become
complicit?
Dallas, just last summer: I'm standing beside a man

(God, he must be
nineteen) who wears our state upon

his sleeve and feels its boots walk him wherever it says
he's needed. Our airplanes
wait, his lover sobs, TVs
hum like word balloons above us; in them five men speak

of foreign threats,
their bodies framed by pillar after

pillar. Hours pass, the soldier sighs, I read a book
to keep from looking.
I wish that none of this were
true, that the heartland grew more question marks and stopped

taking the bullets
it's been given. As it now stands

my mother's last best Ohio friend answers every
Apache crash (her son

pilots them) with Valium,
dissent expends its last nuanced breath, and word after

word is hollowed out
(*patriot, terrorist*), strung into

the same delaying thread, the great deferment
of climax.
            Yesterday, I lost an hour to a Caravaggio—
it was Judith, her arms awash in blood, cradling

the head, the half-bit
            tongue, of Holofernes. The maid

is there, the knife glints silver, scarlet. Here is the part
that's missing:
            her tease, his hushed *oh please*,
the slow verbal seduction, which despite her looks, his lust,

remains the sharper
            weapon. Holofernes must have known

that this was wrong, that somehow this was what she wanted.
Still, he walked to the slaughter—
            M. Tulli, quid agis?
In Rome they're roiling in the death throes

of their Republic.
            Within the month Catiline's five

conspirators are dead, choked by the State outside
the Forum. Their leader lives
            another few weeks (maybe
hears Cicero elected *pater patriae*) before

he's carved up
                    with his legion. Do we know
now where this sentence goes? Can we translate *auctorem
sceleris*? Somewhere a typewriter
                                        stalls; some guns
are jammed but smoking. I have not placed

one useful word between them.

NOTES

Throughout this book I have made varying use of the Latin corpus: bor-
rowings, quotations, adaptations, and loose translations (whole or part).
Overall I have taken great liberties with the original texts, treating each
as an occasion to mold, hybridize, or expand my own voice. The poems
that most closely resemble their predecessors are the Propertius section
of "On the Hills of Perusia," as well as "His Doctor, His Fever" and "A
Priest to Paul Russus" (both from "Songs of Sickness"). Source material
and other notes are as follows:

"Fellini's Cabiria": Roland Barthes is quoted from "Leaving the Movie
Theatre."

"Vitruvian Man": line six paraphrases a sentence from Leonardo Da
Vinci's notebooks. I am indebted to Adam Gopnik's review of two recent
Da Vinci biographies: *Leonardo* and *Leonardo Da Vinci: Flights of the
Mind* (*The New Yorker*: January 17, 2005).

"Songs of Sickness": All Latin sources can be found in *Jesuit Latin Poets
of the 17th and 18th Centuries*, edited by James J. Mertz, S.J. and John
P. Murphy, S.J. in collaboration with Jozef Ijsewijn, Bolchazy-Carducci
Publishers, 1989.

"Fellini's Satyricon": Along with texts cited within the poem, J.P.
Sullivan's translation, notes, and introduction to *The Satyricon*,
(Penguin, 1977) were of great use. "Braund et. al" refers to Susanna
Morton Braund, editor of *Juvenal: Satires Book I*, Cambridge UP, 1996.

"Fellini's Roma": All information about Rome comes from the
Encyclopedia Britannica or *Roma* itself.

"On the Hills of Perusia": for the original Propertius see W.A. Camps's
edition of the *Monobiblos Properti*, Cambridge UP, 1961.

"Thanatology": For the science of thanatology see the *Britannica*'s Macropedia, vol. 16.

"Period": In November 63 BCE, nearing the end of his one-year consulship, Marcus Tullius Cicero uncovered a conspiracy that had been fomenting under a political rival, Catiline. In a series of four orations, he outlined the charges. *In L. Catilinam Oratio Prima* 254-258 is a typical periodic sentence: "Marcus Tulli, what are you doing? Will you allow this man—whom you know to be an enemy, whom you foresee leading wars, a commander in fact, expected in the enemy camps, an author of crimes, the conspiracy's leader, and a recruiter of slaves—to leave; won't it seem that instead of exiling him from Rome, you welcomed him inside it?" (translation mine).

Also Available from saturnalia books:

FAULKNER'S ROSARY by Sarah Vap

GURLESQUE: THE NEW GRRLY, GROTESQUE, BURLESQUE POETICS
edited by Arielle Greenberg & Lara Glenum

THE LITTLE OFFICE OF THE IMMACULATE CONCEPTION by Martha Silano
WINNER OF THE SATURNALIA BOOKS POETRY PRIZE 2010

PERSONIFICATION by Margaret Rhonda
WINNER OF THE SATURNALIA BOOKS POETRY PRIZE 2009

TO THE BONE by Sebastian Agudelo
WINNER OF THE SATURNALIA BOOKS POETRY PRIZE 2008

FAMOUS LAST WORDS by Catherine Pierce
WINNER OF THE SATURNALIA BOOKS POETRY PRIZE 2007

DUMMY FIRE by Sarah Vap
WINNER OF THE SATURNALIA BOOKS POETRY PRIZE 2006

CORRESPONDENCE by Kathleen Graber
WINNER OF THE SATURNALIA BOOKS POETRY PRIZE 2005

THE BABIES by Sabrina Orah Mark
WINNER OF THE SATURNALIA BOOKS POETRY PRIZE 2004

VELLEITY'S SHADE
Poems by Star Black / Artwork by Bill Knott
ARTIST/POET COLLABORATION SERIES NUMBER SIX

AND MANY MORE...

OTHER ROMES was printed using the fonts New Century Schoolbook and
ITC Avant Garde.

www.saturnaliabooks.com